S0-AIE-795

My First Book

About me

Felicity Brooks

Me? I wrote the words.

Me? I painted the pictures.

Illustrated by Mar Ferrero

Designed by Francesca Allen

Me? I designed the book.

Contents

Usborne Quicklinks

To visit websites with video clips, activities and things to make and do, go to
www.usborne.com/quicklinks and type in the keywords "first book about me"
We recommend that children are supervised while using the internet.

I am me and you are you

Add the missing picture stickers.

This book is all about me!

and me

and us

I'm Anisha. I live at home with my grandad. Who do you live with?

I'm Joe. I like reading about animals. What do you like doing?

We are Oscar and Oliver. We look the same but we like different things.

and me

and me

and you!

and me!

My name is Kirsty. I have red hair and freckles. I like jumping rope.

My family calls me Mo. I have black hair and I like math and dancing.

Hello! I'm Valentine and I love to draw. Can you draw a picture of yourself?

Everyone is different

Take a look at all the people around you. No one is just the same as you.

Can you add the missing picture stickers?

Some are GRUMPY, and some are HAPPY.

Some are short and W I D E.

Some are tall and thin.

Some are YOUNG.
Some are OLD.
Some are in between.

Some wear cool glasses.

What do you look like?

meow

Some have pale skin, some have dark skin, some are in between.
Some have long hair, some have short hair. . . and some have no hair at all!

3

Me and my day

This is what I do on a school day.

Anisha

After I wake up, I use the toilet, wash my hands and brush my teeth.

I brush my hair and put on my school clothes. I can dress myself.

After I've eaten my breakfast and had a drink, I feed my fish.

I make sure I have what I need for school and I put on my coat and shoes.

I always walk to school with Grandad. We cross the street at the crosswalk.

At school we hang up our coats before we go into our classroom.

In our classroom we do drawing, writing, puzzles, reading and numbers.

At playtime we go outside. I like to play with my friends Kirsty and Carla.

Match the sticker labels to the pictures to show what Anisha does in the afternoon.

walk home

play in the park

dance lesson

TV time

mealtime

bathtime

story time

bedtime

5

Me and my feelings

Feelings can change during the day. How do you think each child feels in this picture?

Match the sticker labels to the pictures to show how each child feels.

What do you think made Mo feel happy?
What makes you feel happy? When do you feel upset?

Which is which?

Joe has drawn some faces to show different feelings. Can you match the sticker faces to the words?

Match my pictures to the words.

angry

happy

worried

excited

scared

sad

Saying sorry

If you do or say something that makes somebody feel sad or bad, you hurt their feelings. You can say "sorry" to make them feel better.

You broke my toy!

I'm sorry!

7

Me and my body

Each part of my body has a name. Do you know all these?

head

finger

knee

chest

Kirsty

toe

neck

Match the sticker labels to the pictures.

hair

tummy

elbow

foot

shoulder

bottom

leg

hand

8

Mo and his friends are pointing to different parts of their faces. Can you match the sticker labels to the pictures?

eye

ear

nose

cheek

mouth

lip

eyebrow

chin

How do you think these children feel in each picture? Add a sticker label to match each one.

hot

cold

sick

sleepy

Me and my clothes

Look at all the clothes below and help Valentine choose what to wear on...

I can get dressed by myself. Can you?

1 a sunny day

2 a rainy day

3 a snowy day

skirt

raincoat

tights

scarf

sunhat

boots

t-shirt

sandals

gloves

jeans

sneakers

coat

sweater

hat

socks

shorts

10

Use the clothes stickers to finish dressing Valentine and her friends for...

swimming

painting

a party

dancing

soccer

bedtime

11

Me and my food

Your body needs different kinds
of food each day to stay healthy.

You need bread, rice,
potatoes or pasta
to give you
energy.

You need plenty
of vegetables
and fruit.

Eggs, meat, fish,
beans, nuts and
seeds help you grow.

You need cheese,
milk and yogurt for
healthy bones and teeth.

Water or
milk is best
to drink.

You don't need many of these
sweet foods as they are bad
for your teeth and body.

What I like to eat

Use the stickers to give these hungry children the meals they like best.

Thanks! That looks yummy.

chicken and salad

vegetable stir-fry and rice

pasta and shrimp

Thank you!

spaghetti and tomato sauce

fish sticks and peas

Can you draw a picture of the meal you like best?

My family and friends

Mo has made a book about his family and friends. Add the stickers to match the missing pictures to the words he has written.

My best friend's name is Joe. He makes me laugh all the time.

Hannah takes care of us when my mom and step-dad are working.

My cousin Ben is very tall and he plays the guitar.

My step-dad is a firefighter but he always burns the toast!

This is a drawing of my cat. Her name is Fluff.

Our dog Max

My mom wears funny skirts.

Our neighbors, Doug and Greg, are very nice.

Bella, my baby sister, eats mushy food.

My teacher is Miss Sanchez. She has spiky hair and likes to wear big boots.

My gran has a pet snake. She calls him Gorgeous George.

If you made a book about your family and friends, who would you put in it? Who are the special people who help you in your life?

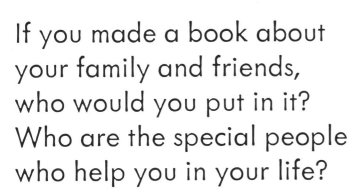

My little brother loves his pirate hat. He wears it all the time.

What I can do
Your body can do all kinds of amazing things.

climb

wave

drink

sit

cry

stand

talk

b-b-bird!

walk

count

play

jump

read

Which of these can you do?

run

KEEP OFF THE GRASS

16

My senses

Your five senses help you find out about the world around you.

With your eyes you can...

SEE.

That's soooo slimy!

With your skin you can...

TOUCH.

Mmmmm!

With your nose you can...

SMELL.

Yum!

With your mouth you can...

TASTE.

BANG! BANG!

Wow!

With your ears you can...

HEAR.

What a pretty fish!

Add the sticker labels to this page to show which sense is which.

What am I good at?

People like to do different things and some people can do things better than others.
Do you know what you are good at?

Oscar likes baking cakes and decorating them.

Anisha writes exciting adventure stories.

Valentine is very good at drawing and painting.

Oliver can do all kinds of tricks on his skateboard.

Mo is the best at math. He likes singing, too.

Joe takes great photos of plants and animals.

Here are some other things the friends like to do.
Put a star sticker next to the ones you'd like to do too.

eating ice cream ☐

riding a bike ☐

reading ☐

taking care of pets ☐

running fast ☐

playing computer games ☐

dancing ☐

collecting things ☐

judo ☐

swimming ☐

climbing a tree ☐

jumping rope ☐

playing soccer ☐

bouncing ☐

doing cartwheels ☐

We like looking at the stars.

Growing and changing

When you were a baby, you could only do a few things, but as you grow up, your body grows and you learn to do more and more.

When Joe was a tiny baby, he could sleep, poop, pee, cry and drink milk.

Then he learned to sit and eat food. He grew teeth and started to feed himself.

Next he learned how to crawl and then to stand up. Soon he could walk.

DUCK!

He began to say a few words and then lots. (Now he knows thousands!)

He learned to use the potty and then he started to use the toilet.

Soon he could run, jump, dance, climb and say some numbers and colors.

At school he is learning to read and write and to do math.

BRAINTON BIG SCHOOL

When he's older, he'll be able to go to school all by himself.

Joe Age 1
Joe Age 2
Joe Age 3

One day he might go to college and then become a dad himself and help take care of a tiny baby.

21

What do I need?

The friends are talking about things they want and things they need. Do you know which is which?

Clothes and shoes to keep me warm and dry

Friends to play with

Someone to help me learn the things I need to know

Things to keep my brain busy and help me learn stuff

Somewhere to bathe and use the toilet

Clean water and food to keep my body healthy

A doctor to help me if I am sick.

Someone to take care of me

Exercise and fresh air

A safe, warm, dry place to live and sleep

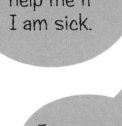

Match one sticker label to each page.

22

All about me

This is a page of a book Kirsty made all about herself. What would you put in a book about you?

I love my sister, Sophie.

Name: Kirsty Trellis

I like jumping rope.

Pets: Bob (dog)

Bob has a waggy tail.

Things I don't like

peas

slugs

smelly shoes

My school: Mesa Elementary School

FROGS ARE THE BEST!

My friends: Anisha, Mo, Joe.

My hobbies: painting and drawing